EXPLORE THE U.S.A.

MISSISSIPPI

Pamela McDowell

www.av2books.com

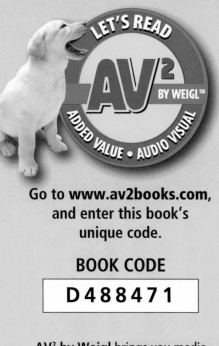

Go to **www.av2books.com**, and enter this book's unique code.

BOOK CODE

D488471

AV² by Weigl brings you media enhanced books that support active learning.

AV² provides enriched content that supplements and complements this book. Weigl's AV² books strive to create inspired learning and engage young minds in a total learning experience.

Your AV² Media Enhanced books come alive with...

Audio
Listen to sections of the book read aloud.

Video
Watch informative video clips.

Embedded Weblinks
Gain additional information for research.

Try This!
Complete activities and hands-on experiments.

Key Words
Study vocabulary, and complete a matching word activity.

Quizzes
Test your knowledge.

Slide Show
View images and captions, and prepare a presentation.

... and much, much more!

Published by AV² by Weigl
350 5th Avenue, 59th Floor
New York, NY 10118
Website: www.av2books.com   www.weigl.com

Library of Congress Cataloging-in-Publication Data
McDowell, Pamela.
 Mississippi / Pamela McDowell.
    p. cm. -- (Explore the u.s.a.)
Includes bibliographical references and index.
ISBN 978-1-61913-367-9 (hard cover : alk. paper)
1. Mississippi--Juvenile literature. I. Title.
F341.3.M33 2012
976.2--dc23
                          2012015092

Printed in the United States of America in North Mankato, Minnesota
1 2 3 4 5 6 7 8 9 16 15 14 13 12

052012
WEP040512

Project Coordinator: Karen Durrie
Art Director: Terry Paulhus

Weigl acknowledges Getty Images as the primary image supplier for this title.

MISSISSIPPI

Contents

3

This is Mississippi.
It is called the Magnolia State.
A magnolia is a flower
that grows in Mississippi.

This is the shape of Mississippi. It is in the south part of the United States. Mississippi borders four states and the Gulf of Mexico.

Where is Mississippi?

Canada

N
W · E
S

Pacific Ocean

United States

Atlantic Ocean

Mexico

Gulf of Mexico

The Mississippi River runs through the state.

Hernando de Soto was one of the first explorers to come to Mississippi. He came on a ship from Spain.

The Spanish explorers were looking for gold.

The magnolia is the Mississippi state flower. The magnolia has a sweet smell.

The Mississippi state seal has an eagle, arrows, and an olive branch.

The olive branch and arrows stand for peace and war.

This is the state flag of Mississippi. It is red, white, and blue.

The flag has stripes and a cross with stars.

The state animal of Mississippi is the white-tailed deer. There are almost two million white-tailed deer in Mississippi.

Young white-tailed deer have spots.

This is the biggest city in Mississippi. It is named Jackson. It is the capital city of Mississippi.

Jackson has 19 museums.

Oil is found in Mississippi. Oil is used to make fuel, plastics, and chemicals.

Mississippi has more than 2,000 oil wells.

The Mississippi River is the longest river in North America. People come to Mississippi to take riverboat tours and see the many sights along the river.

MISSISSIPPI FACTS

These pages provide detailed information that expands on the interesting facts found in the book. These pages are intended to be used by adults as a learning support to help young readers round out their knowledge of each state in the *Explore the U.S.A.* series.

Pages 4–5

Mississippi is named after the Mississippi River. The word *Mississippi* comes from the Chippewa Indians. It means "big river." The magnolia tree grows throughout Mississippi. Magnolia flowers can be white, yellow, or pink.

Pages 6–7

On December 10, 1817, Mississippi became the 20th state to join the United States. Mississippi borders Louisiana, Arkansas, Tennessee, and Alabama. Most of Mississippi's western border is created by the Mississippi River. The southern edge of Mississippi touches the Gulf of Mexico. This area is called the Gulf Coast. The Mississippi River and Gulf Coast are important for shipping goods to other parts of the United States and around the world.

Pages 8–9

Hernando de Soto was the first European to discover the Mississippi River in 1541. He came looking for gold and silver, but he did not find either in Mississippi. Other European explorers arrived in the Mississippi area more than 100 years later. René-Robert Cavelier, Sieur de La Salle, claimed the Mississippi region for France in 1682.

Pages 10–11

In 1900, schoolchildren voted to select the Mississippi state flower. The magnolia received more than half of the votes. A magnolia tree can grow up to 102 feet (31 meters) high. The Mississippi state seal has been used since 1798. The eagle holds an olive branch to symbolize peace and arrows to show the power to wage war.

Pages 12–13

The colors of the wide bars on the Mississippi flag represent the national colors of the United States. The blue cross with 13 white stars is referred to as the Confederate battle flag or the Union Square. The 13 stars represent the first 13 states that formed the United States.

Pages 14–15

A white-tailed deer can run 40 miles (64 kilometers) per hour and jump 9-foot (2.7-meter) fences. A male deer is called a buck, and a female deer is called a doe. Bucks have antlers that fall off and grow again each year. Eleven states have the white-tailed deer as their state animal.

Pages 16–17

Jackson was named after Andrew Jackson, who was the seventh president of the United States. The city has a population of about 175,000 people. The Dixie National Livestock Show and Rodeo is held every February. It runs for 24 days and features events such as bull riding, roping, and barrel racing.

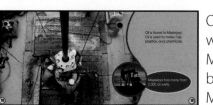

Pages 18–19

Oil is the most valuable resource in Mississippi. The state has oil wells on land and in the Gulf of Mexico. Shipyards in Pascagoula, Mississippi, build oil tankers used to transport the oil. Shrimp, broiler chickens, and cotton are other goods important to the Mississippi economy.

Pages 20–21

The Mississippi River is 2,350 miles (3,780 kilometers) long. It begins at Lake Itasca in Minnesota, and it exits into the Gulf of Mexico. Riverboats have large paddlewheels at the back. They are a common sight on the Mississippi River. People can take cruises and stop at different points to learn about the state's history.

KEY WORDS

Research has shown that as much as 65 percent of all written material published in English is made up of 300 words. These 300 words cannot be taught using pictures or learned by sounding them out. They must be recognized by sight. This book contains 52 common sight words to help young readers improve their reading fluency and comprehension. This book also teaches young readers several important content words, such as proper nouns. These words are paired with pictures to aid in learning and improve understanding.

Page	Sight Words First Appearance
4	a, grows, in, is, it, state, that, the, this
7	and, four, of, part, river, runs, though, where
8	came, come, first, for, from, he, on, one, to, was, were
11	an, has
12	white, with
15	almost, animal, are, have, there, two, young
16	city, named
19	found, make, more, than, used, wells
20	along, many, people, see, take

Page	Content Words First Appearance
4	flower, magnolia, Mississippi
7	Gulf of Mexico, shape, United States
8	explorers, gold, Hernando de Soto, ship, Spain
11	arrows, eagle, olive branch, peace, seal, smell, war
12	cross, flag, stars, stripes
15	spots, white-tailed deer
16	Jackson, museums
19	chemicals, fuel, oil, plastics
20	North America, sights, tours